First World War
and Army of Occupation
War Diary
France, Belgium and Germany

17 DIVISION
Divisional Troops
80 Brigade Royal Field Artillery
14 July 1915 - 31 August 1916

WO95/1991/5

The Naval & Military Press Ltd
www.nmarchive.com
Published in association with The National Archives

Published by

The Naval & Military Press Ltd

Unit 10 Ridgewood Industrial Park,
Uckfield, East Sussex,
TN22 5QE England
Tel: +44 (0) 1825 749494

www.naval-military-press.com

www.nmarchive.com

This diary has been reprinted in facsimile from the original. Any imperfections are inevitably reproduced and the quality may fall short of modern type and cartographic standards.

© **Crown Copyright**
Images reproduced by permission of The National Archives, London, England, 2015.

Contents

Document type	Place/Title	Date From	Date To
Heading	WO95/1991/5		
Heading	17th Division 80th Brigade R.F.A. Jly 1915-Aug 1916 Bde Broken Up 31/8/16		
Heading	17 Division 80th Brigade R.F.A. Vol I 14-31-7-15 Vol		
War Diary	Winchester	14/07/1915	14/07/1915
War Diary	Southampton	14/07/1915	14/07/1915
War Diary	Le Harve	15/07/1915	15/07/1915
War Diary	Wizernes	16/07/1915	16/07/1915
War Diary	Lynde	18/07/1915	18/07/1915
War Diary	Fletre	19/07/1915	31/07/1915
Heading	17th Division 80th Brigade R.F.A. Vol II From 31 Jly To 31aug 15		
War Diary	Fletre	31/07/1915	31/07/1915
War Diary	Boeschepe	03/08/1915	04/08/1915
War Diary	Dickebusch	05/08/1915	16/08/1915
War Diary	Boescheppe	17/08/1915	31/08/1915
Heading	War Diary 80 Bde Rfa		
Operation(al) Order(s)	17th Division R.A. Order No 8	08/08/1915	08/08/1915
Heading	17th Division 80th Bde. R.F.A. Vol III Sept 15		
War Diary	Boeschepe	01/09/1915	06/09/1915
War Diary	Dickebusch	06/09/1915	22/09/1915
War Diary	Kemmel	23/09/1915	23/09/1915
War Diary	Kemmel Village	25/09/1915	29/09/1915
Diagram etc	To Shoe:- Telephone Communication 80th. F.A.B		
Miscellaneous	Intelligence Report No 2 Group:- From 6 Am 28.9.15 To 6pm 28.9.15	28/09/1915	28/09/1915
Heading	17th Division 80th Bde. R.F.A. Vol 4 Oct 15		
War Diary	Kemmel Village	30/09/1915	30/09/1915
War Diary	Boeschepe	02/10/1915	02/10/1915
War Diary	St. Sylvestre Cappel	08/10/1915	08/10/1915
War Diary	Ypres	22/10/1915	24/10/1915
War Diary	Zillebeke Lake	24/10/1915	31/10/1915
Miscellaneous	B 80 Bde R.F.A.		
Heading	The Office i/c Adjutants Generals Office Base		
Miscellaneous	C 80th Bde R.F.A.		
Miscellaneous	D 80 Bde R.F.A.		
Heading	17th Division 80th Bde R.F.A. Nov 15		
War Diary	Zillebeke Etang I 15a 11	01/11/1915	30/11/1915
Heading	17th Div 80th Bde R.F.A. Vol: 6		
War Diary	Zillebeke Etang I 15d 11	05/12/1915	30/12/1915
Heading	80th Bde. R.F.A. Vol: 7 Jan 16		
War Diary	Zillebeke Etang I 15d 11	01/01/1916	11/01/1916
War Diary	Arneke	11/01/1916	12/01/1916
War Diary	Bonningues	13/01/1916	31/01/1916
War Diary	Bonningues	01/02/1916	11/02/1916
War Diary	Dickebusch Night	11/02/1916	16/03/1916
War Diary	Le Kreul	12/03/1916	23/03/1916
War Diary	Armentieres	23/03/1916	31/03/1916
War Diary	Armentieres	12/04/1916	19/04/1916
War Diary	Acquin	20/05/1916	11/06/1916

War Diary	Gibraltar	24/06/1916	28/06/1916
Heading	17th Div. XV. Corps. War Diary Headquarters. 80th Brigade, R.F.A. July (29.6.16-31.7.16) 1916		
War Diary	Gibralter	29/06/1916	01/07/1916
War Diary	Carnoy Map. R.E.F. Amiens 17 I.J	03/07/1916	15/07/1916
War Diary	Ref Map Longueval 22a5.2	15/07/1916	23/07/1916
War Diary	Dernancourt E. 14 & 22	24/07/1916	31/07/1916
Miscellaneous	Head Quarters 17 Divisional Artillery	26/07/1916	26/07/1916
Heading	17th Divisional Artillery 80th Brigade Royal Field Artillery August 1916 Casualties-Animals Personnel ammunition expenditure.		
War Diary	Montauban	01/08/1916	19/08/1916
War Diary	Amiens 17	20/08/1916	23/08/1916
War Diary	Henu D13b D13c	24/08/1916	31/08/1916
War Diary	Gaudiempre D1a & D1b	31/08/1916	31/08/1916

W205/199(5)

17TH DIVISION

80TH BRIGADE R.F.A.
JLY 1915 - AUG 1916

Bde. Broken up 31/8/16

14th Division.

80th Brigade R.F.A.

Vol. I.

14-31-7-15

Aug '16

13/6/96

WAR DIARY
INTELLIGENCE SUMMARY
(Erase heading not required.)

Army Form C. 2118

80th Brigade R.F.A.
17 Division —
2nd New Army.

Place	Date	Hour	Summary of Events and Information	Remarks and references to Appendices
			MAP. BELGIUM. Sheet HAZEBROUCK 5A. Scale 1/40000.	
WINCHESTER	14/7/15	3.45 pm	H.Q. Brigade proceeded march route to Southampton. Bde. O. No 38.	
S.HAMPTON	14/7/15	6.15 pm	Sailed inclusive coact. Embarked on S.S. Manchester Importer.	pm
LE HAVRE	15/7/15	12 mn	arrived off HAVRE 4.30 am 15/7/15.	
			Disembarked. B.C. + Bde. Am. Col. proceeded N° 6 Rest Camp. D to HALLE in trucks.	
WIZERNES	16/7/15	5.30 pm	remainder entrained at GARE DES MERCHANDISE. and left at 10 pm.	
			Detrained march route to AYROULT. to Billets. Various times of arrival	
LYNDE	18/7/15	9.30	Marched } Billets + WAVRANS. (c + D)	
		3.45	arrived }	
FLETRE	19/7/15	10 am	marched } Billets	
	20	4 pm	arrived }	
			Brigade was inspected by 20 Lt Genl. HERBERT PLUMER. Capt + Adjt. C.F.K. MARSHALL RFA. joined 1st Yorks Bde. R.F.A. 2t + Adjt. H.MORGAN. joined.	
FLETRE.	31/7/15	10 am.	Remained in Billet at this place, completing training, all officers went to the front, and visited the part of the line occupied by 28th Division, very valuable experience gained by so doing.	

Own Column,

The undermentioned are present with the Brigade at date:—

Bde. Hd Qrs
Capt: H. CAYLEY WEBSTER

A. Bty.
2/Lt: A. FILLINGHAM. Lt. Colonel G.A. CARDEN. Major A.H. HARPUR.
"   M.W. SMITH   Lt. + Adjt: H. MORGAN.   Lieut: W.H. GOSSE.

B Bty
Major P.H. PRESTON. Capt: H.J. CANNAN.
Lieut: D.C.G. SHARP.   2/Lt: C.B.F. PARKINSON.

C. Bty
Capt: H.J. CANNAN.   Capt: R.W. BELL
2/Lt: C.B.F. PARKINSON.   2/Lt: T.D. FAIRGRIEVE

"   H.W. STRANGMAN.   2/Lt: R.G. SOUTHEY. 2/Lt: R.S. PARKES.   2/Lt: P. FERGUSON.   —"   G.B.A. LANDSDOWNE. —" R.M. BOWMAN.
"   R.G. SOUTHEY.   S.M. (W.O.) D. BEHAN.   —" E.S. HOUGHTON. —" W.J. BARNATO.   —" A.W. DAVIES. 2/Lt: T.C. JACQUES.
+ 148 NCO's + men.   and. 36. NCO's + men.   + 130 NCO's + men.   + 131 NCO's + men.   + 130 NCO's + men.   + 130 NCO's + men.

H.Morgan Adjt 80 Pde.

Lt Colonel R.F.A.
Commanding 80 Brigade R.F.A.

121/6607

14th Division

80th Brigade R.F.A.
Vol: II
from 31 July to 31 Aug. 15

8/15

A. Morgan. Lt. & Adjutant.

WAR DIARY
of
INTELLIGENCE SUMMARY
(Erase heading not required.)

Army Form C. 2118

80th Brigade R.F.A.
17th Division
2nd New Army.

Ref. Map BELGIUM. HAZEBROUCK Sheet 5A 1/100,000.

Place	Date	Hour	Summary of Events and Information	Remarks and references to Appendices
FLETRE	31/7/15	4 pm	Orders received from Div HQ. to march at 10 pm. to BOESCHEPE. March completed by last unit of Bde about 2 am. 1-8-15. All work, Billets, good men for march; passed through METEREN. Country flat; undulating weather fine. Could see the "Line" by flares and bursting shell.	fm.
BOESCHEPE	3rd 8-15	3.30 pm	Small arm section of Bde A.C. proceeded into action attached under 2/Lt. Fillingham. (FILLINGHAM.) at 11 pm for attachment to H.2nd F.A. Bde A.C. to supply small arms ammunition to 50th & 51st Inf. Bdes. The multiplicity of Returns and ever increasing correspondence does not appear to agree with F.S. Regs. Part II. which says correspondence should be cut to a minimum.	fm.
		4 pm	Colonel receives orders to proceed to D.H.Q. R.A. with his B.C's to select positions for his Batteries in the line. There appears to be new positions entirely - returned about 10.30 pm to BOESCHEPE.	fm.
— " —	6/8/15	4 am	Revival units are behind the line, in reserve, would appear to be harder on officers, other ranks, and horses. Bde has to find 30 prs of wheelers daily under an officer - Dragging parties of 30 N.C.O.'s and men per Bty, with all officers, proceed to prepare gun pits in vicinity of DICKEBUSCH. The guns to be taken up under cover of darkness tonight. The list of officers the names of Medical officers and Veterinary Officers were omitted, now entered. M.O. Lieut. J. L. DIGBY. (T.C.) R.A.M.C. M.B.Ch.M. (SYD) V.O. Lieut Howard Jones. A.V.C.(T.C.)	fm. fm.

A/Morgan Lt + Adjutant 80th Brigade R.F.A. Army Form C. 2118
17th Division
2nd New Army

WAR DIARY
INTELLIGENCE SUMMARY
(Erase heading not required.)

Place	Date	Hour	Summary of Events and Information	Remarks and references to Appendices
DICKEBUSCH	5/8/15	4 am	Reference Map: BELGIUM and FRANCE ("B" Series) Sheet 28. S.W. Scale 20,000. All Batteries safely into action, very well dug in by 4 am, many aeroplane scares. A uniform system of signals by whistle is regarded for use throughout the army. At present some unit blows 1 blast on appearance of 'plane, others 2. First round fired about 4 pm by "D" Bty. all Batteries fired a few rounds each. for registration purposes. Have fairly good ridge in Square N.W. but there is a gun to nearly every 30 yards. Village of DICKEBUSCH main knocked about, church very much so, is a ruin. Tower completely demolished by German heavy guns. shell. Officers, N.C.O. and men very keen, lost all boredom, but inclined to be a little casual. A good deal of mooching and many flares during the night 5"—6".	fm
-"-	6/8/15	10 am	Everything very quiet. weather fine, mild.	
		4.30 pm	First man wounded. the house occupied as a billet and telephone exchange by Hd Qrs rather heavily shelled by German 6" Shrapnel, one of the buf telep hones hit in the head by a piece pshell, G. Fleet. moved to another part of village in the morning.	fm
-"-	7/8/15	10 am	Registration of Targets carried out by aeroplane observation. Colonel Cardew (CARDEW) placed in command of Group "A" Artillery - Consisting of 80th R.F.A. Bde. 2 Guns 15pdr D/78. 2. 4.5"how" of C/81.	fm

WAR DIARY
or
INTELLIGENCE SUMMARY

(Erase heading not required.)

Army Form C. 2118

H. Morgan Lt + Adjutant

80th Brigade R.F.A.
17th Division
2nd New Army

Place	Date	Hour	Summary of Events and Information	Remarks and references to Appendices
DICKEBUSH	9 & 15	2 am.	Ref. Map Sheets 28 + 27. Scale 1:20000 and 1:40000. "A" Group. appointed as Counter Batteries to assist in attack on HOOGE. Enemy Trenches recently lost by us. Bombardment commenced at 2-35 am. and continued firing in bursts, till 9 am., in conjunction with other groups. "A" Group began at 2-45 am. a total of 638 Shrapnel and 167 High Explosive was fired. No aeroplane observation was available during this attack. The attack was reported as quite successful. and in the afternoon B/13 Commenced to fire again at a slower rate.	Copy of orders to "Y" Group attached
"	"	11-12 noon.	No. 2 & No. 3. Guns wounded rather severely in head by shrapnel. German guns fairly busy - but not doing much damage. Orders received to continue fire whenever German guns are active in direction of HOOGE.	ditto
"	"	TO. 16-8. 9 am.	Orders received to withdraw personnel to back billets - guns to be left in the line, ready to be manned. Very heavy shelling of DICKEBUSCH by German 8" & H.E. on 14th - G. Standfast - About 20 casualties - G. Standfast and Dr Cunningham wounded, the latter severely, artillery fairly active both sides nearly every day. N.C.O's and men cause casualties by being too curious - going out to see the damage after a shell burst - Major E.H. HARPUR posted to 2nd Army - pending promotion - Captain H.A.S. CHAMIER 3rd Lahore Div. assumes command of A/80 Lt. D.C.S. SHARP Bn wounded in DICKEBUSH, R.E. DUMP. Shrapnel Arm	

WAR DIARY
or
INTELLIGENCE SUMMARY

(Erase heading not required.)

Army Form C. 2118

Morgan Lt & Adjutant
80th Brigade R.F.A.
17th Division
2nd New Army

Place	Date	Hour	Summary of Events and Information	Remarks and references to Appendices
DOES=SHEPPE	17/8/15	11 am	Ref. Map. Sheet 28 & 27. Scale 1:20000 & 1:40000. A position selected for a forward gun emplacement, work commenced on 16/7/5. Colonel and O.C. B/ij go to vicinity of HELLEBAST. (HELL BLAST CORNER) to select gun positions for G.H.Q.2. N.C.O. and men were not eager to leave their guns behind and come to back billets.	Atts.
"	20/8/15	noon	The forward gun was taken up and placed in position last night. to N.6.c.1.7. The gun is to enfilade Enemy Trenches in O.2.6.	Atts.
"	28/8/15	"	"A" Battery ordered to dig in position in 28th Division Area, so as to be able to bring enfilade fire on to enemy Trenches running parallel to 17th Division's front. Position selected N.10.c.7.1.	
"	31/8/15	9 am	"A" Battery position taken up on night of 27/8. "B" Battery position to be taken up on the South Eastern bank take up One 18 par to a position H.36.a.3.4 on bank of DICKEBUSCH POND. as an anti-aircraft gun, in conjunction with NAVAL AIRCRAFT BATTERY.	Atts.

Morgan Lt Colonel R.F.A.
Commanding 80 Bde R.F.A.

War Diary
50 Bde RFA

SECRET.   17 Div R.A. Order No 8   Copy 1

8/8/15

I. The 17 Div are to make a diversion on a front of 250 yds each side of PICCADILLY FM to-night.

II. The Artillery will assist by bombarding as follows:—

(a) Guns to take part — R. Group — A.B.C. Batteries 78. F.A.B.
 2 guns D/78
L. Group. 2 guns 29 + 45 + 36 Batteries R.F.A.   2 — " C/81 (How)

(b) Front to be engaged.

R. Group — N.E. Corner of BOIS QUARANTE to PICCADILLY FM (inclusive) : front line and support trenches.

L. Group — PICCADILLY FM (exclusive) to Road junction in O.2.c.7.1 : front line and support trenches.

(c) Phases of Bombardment.

	From	To	Rate of fire
1st Phase	2.35 a.m.	2.50 a.m.	1 round per gun per min
	2.50 a.m.	2.55 a.m.	
2nd Phase	2.55 a.m.	3.5 a.m.	2 " " " "
3rd Phase	3.5 a.m.	3.15 a.m.	1 " " " "

During 3rd Phase raise range 200x.

(d) The 2 forward guns 42nd F.A.B. and 2 m.g. guns will co-operate under instructions to be given separately to O.C. L/16 Group.

(attachment of Ann.)

Sheet 2

III. Allotment of Amn

R. Group. 18 pr. Shrapnel 560   HE. 70
         4.5"   "   45   " 45
L   "   18 pr   "   230   " 30
     "   4.5"   "   45   " 45

This allotment is not to be exceeded.

IV. Signal Time will be circulated from 17 D.A.
Hq at 10 p.m. tonight.

V. Acknowledge

Issued at 1.30 p.m.

J. F. St John Major
B.M. 17. D.A.

131/6920

17th Division

80th Bde: RFA.
Vol: III
Sept. 15

Lt. and Adjt. H. Morgan   80th Brigade R.F.A.   Army Form C. 2118
                                 17th Division
WAR DIARY
INTELLIGENCE SUMMARY
                                 2nd New Army
(Erase heading not required.)

Place	Date	Hour	Summary of Events and Information	Remarks and references to Appendices
			Reference Map Sheet 27 & 28 Scale 1:10,000 & 1:20,000 Belgium.	
BOES- CHEPE	1st to 6th 9/15 6/9/15		Resting. Weather wet, dull.	Hm.
DICKE- BUSCH	6/9/15 to 14/9/15	2 pm	Batteries ordered to open fire again. Enemy Artillery active. Nothing of any importance to report between the dates shown. The Batteries have registered a good many points in the enemy's line, mostly communication trenches behind front line. The anti aircraft gun is reported to have brought down a German 'plane on evening of 10th but report not substantiated. 2nd Lieutenant W.E. KING is posted to the Brigade, and joins Ammn Column on 14th in place of Lt Sharp who was invalided to England wounded. The Bde Hd Qrs moves to N end of village. South end considered too typoa. It was in full view of the WYTSCHAETE RIDGE. "C" Battery were heavily shelled with 8.2 inch Armour piercing shells on 13th between 3 & 4 pm. 42 shells dropped, one was blind, Battery suffered no casualties.	Hm.
-"-	16/9/15 to 22/9/15		Guns remounted in action. but nothing worth recording happened. up to 22nd when orders received to relieve 31st RFA action in front of KEMMEL. These two Brigades and 3rd Brigade are in Corps and the 68th Brigade RFA with 16th Canadian F.A. Battery and a section of 459th Howitzer Battery are supporting the Canadian under orders of C.R.A. Brigade General SHORT. Batteries took up new positions in square N 9, 15, + 16. Tremendous confusion was caused by one FA Bde having to take over two Brigades telephone system and to work in support of two Inf Bde's	Hm.
KEMMEL	23rd			Hm.

Army Form C. 2118

Lt. +Adjt. H Morgan R.fa.   80 Brigade R.fa.

WAR DIARY
or
INTELLIGENCE SUMMARY

(Erase heading not required.)

Instructions regarding War Diaries and Intelligence Summaries are contained in F.S. Regs., Part II. and the Staff Manual respectively. Title Pages will be prepared in manuscript.

17 Division
2nd New Army

Place	Date	Hour	Summary of Events and Information	Remarks and references to Appendices
			Reference Map Sheet 27 + 28 Scale 1/20,000 + 1/40,000 BELGIUM	
KEMMEL VILLAGE	25th	6 am	No 2 Group takes part in Gas + Smoke attack with order to fire on any enemy seen. Enemy in front of this sector KEMMEL HILL FRONT facing WYTSCHAETE very quiet all day. But reports are received from all quarters saying that great attack is universally successful. Orders received to make all arrangements for an advance. Weather very bad, rain commenced on evening of 24th and has kept on.	
KEMMEL VILLAGE	29th	10 am	No more so far. Enemy not very active, morning of 27th 4-30 am six crumps fell in this village, one hit the church. The Brigade is now nothing in conjunction with Canadian 2nd Army. S.O.S. telephone call received by Batteries at various times on 29th & fire opened at once, with successful result in each case. The call S.O.S. was quite unnecessary in each case.	
			30 9/10	

W. Lawrence Lt Colonel R.fa.
Commdg 80 Bde R.fa.

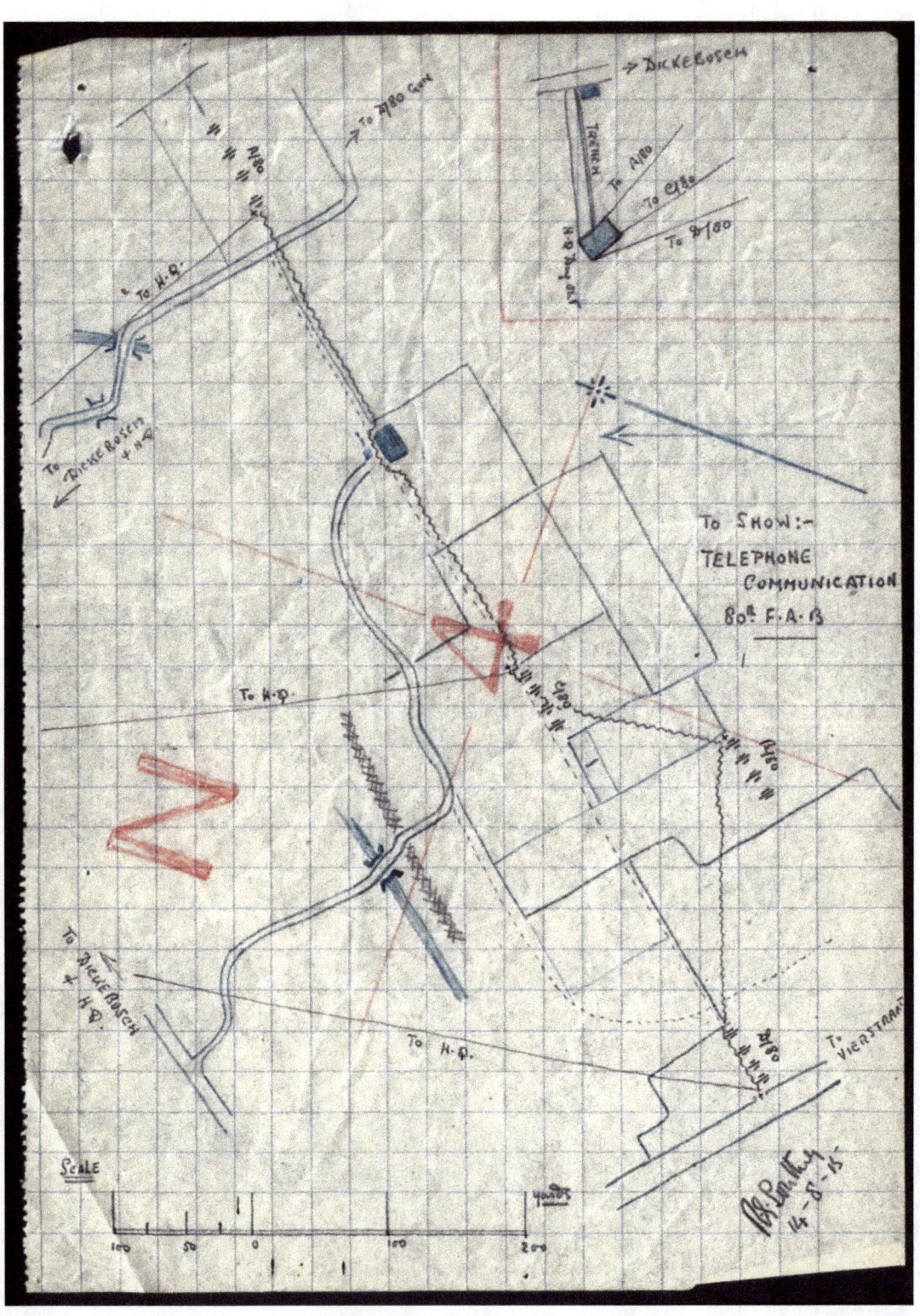

G1/

Intelligence Nº 2 Group:—
From 6 am 28-9-15 to 6 pm 28-9-15.

(1) 2.15 pm.
"A" Bty 50 Bde fired 12 rounds at a working party near O.19.c.7.8., work was stopped —

(2) "J" Trenches were shelled between 10 am & 12 am this morning, B/50 retaliated at urgent request of Infantry — The infantry report that our fire was very effective and the shelling ceased —

8 pm.
28-9-15.

Lt Colonel R.F.A.
Commdg Nº 2 Group.

G.3

Intelligence Report
N° 2 Group Arty
from 6 am 29-9-15 to 6 pm 29-9-15.

(1) About 6 pm following lights were sent up from enemy trench opposite F5. first, 1 white + 3 red. second, 2 white + 2 red —

29/9/15

Madden
Lt Col RA
Commdg 2 Group

This is apparently a signal for arty fire required" but it appears to vary every day — i.e. different signals are sent for the same purpose daily.

121/7593

17th Hussars

So. E. Bde: R.F.A.
Vol 4

Oct 15

K

Lt & Adjutant A morgan RFA. 80th Brigade RFA Army Form C. 2118
17 Division
2nd/New Army

WAR DIARY
or
INTELLIGENCE SUMMARY
(Erase heading not required.)

Summary of Events and Information / Reference Map Sheet 27 & 28 Scale 1/20000 & 1/10000 BELGIUM

Place	Date	Hour	Summary of Events and Information	Remarks and references to Appendices
KEMMEL VILLAGE	30-9-15	9pm	The Brigade is relieved by 2nd Canadian Field Artillery Brigade and proceeds back to BOESCHEPE to old Billets. Move was completed without incident. KEMMEL HILL commands a very interesting observation of about 20 miles in all directions, some very interesting observation was done from the Bde Observing positions, on the hill, while the Batteries were in position. Very useful work could be done in spotting flashes of enemy guns. On a clear day, with a telescope one could see YPRES, HOOGE, COMINES, HOLLEBEKE, MESSINES and WYTSCHAETE.	—
BOES-CHEPE. ST. SYLVESTRE CAPPEL.	2nd/10/15 8/10/15		RESTING. Proceeded by march route to ST SYLVESTRE CAPPEL. On 7-10-15, Capt HAG CHAMIER posted to 79th Bde RFA. Captain M.T.K. O'MALLEY from 1/6 London Bde RFA posted to 80 Bde RFA 16-10-15. Then received orders to relieve 3rd Divl. RESTING to 21-10-15.	—
YPRES.	27/10/15	4.30 pm	Arty, who are in position in the vicinity of ZILLEBEKE ETANG, in the YPRES SALIENT. Relief to be completed by 28-10-15. Guns to be taken over in their positions except two of D/60. Bde Hd Qrs arrive at DERBY MILL a deserted farm just off the DICKEBUSCH - YPRES ROAD. H.24.b.9.3. Hun aeroplane seen flying fairly low under very heavy fire just as party arrives at this farm.	—

1875 Wt. W593/82d 1,000,000 4/15 J.B.C. & A. A.D.S.S./Forms/C.2118.

Lieut & Adjt. Morgan P.S.A. 80th Brigade R.F.A.
17 Division
2nd New Army

WAR DIARY
or
INTELLIGENCE SUMMARY
Army Form C. 2118

(Erase heading not required.)

Place	Date	Hour	Summary of Events and Information	Remarks and references to Appendices
YPRES.	23/10/15	4-30 p.m.	Reference map sheet 27 & 28 Scale 1/20000 & 1/10000 BELGIUM. Aeroplane of yesterday apparently noticed more movement than usual round vicinity of DERBY MILL. This place was very heavily shelled between 5-30pm and 8 pm. Both shrapnel and H.E. were sent and two hits obtained on the house itself, four men wounded two slight and two seriously, pretty bad luck as they were 3 officers servants and two officers Mess Cook. The four took cover in the cellar but were only protected by the board floor overhead. Bde Hd.Qrs moved to Dug outs made in the Bank of ZILLEBEKE ETANG. I.15.d.1.1. Wet weather appears to have set in causing a great deal of trouble into Telephones.	
	24/10/15	→		
ZILLEBEKE LAKE.	24/10/15	4-30 p.m.	Huns commenced to shell the whole area, with both Heavy and Field guns. Hardly any part of the country in vicinity of YPRES that did not receive at least a few shell between 4-30pm 24/10/15 to about 6 pm 25/10/15. C & D Battery were very heavily shelled on afternoon of 25-15 but only two casualties were caused in the Brigade. Life in Dug outs found not to be so uncomfortable as expected.	
	26/10/15		Fairly quiet all day, part of, and Base of two shell picked up, one a 5.9" HE into Triple Driving Band, one a gas shell - the gas would appear to act for quite a long time after shell has exploded. The men who dug up the fuzes suffering from running and burning eyes. Gas has a smell similar to very strong almonds.	

Army Form C. 2118

80 Brigade RFA
17th Division
2nd New Army

WAR DIARY
or
INTELLIGENCE SUMMARY
(Erase heading not required.)

Lt. & Adjutant H Morgan

Place	Date	Hour	Summary of Events and Information	Remarks and references to Appendices
			Reference Map Sheet 28 Scale 1/20000 & 1/1000 BELGIUM	
ZILLEBEKE LAKE. I.15.d.1.1.	29/10/15	2.30 pm to 4 pm	The vicinity of I.15.d.11. very heavily shelled, salvoes of both H.E. and Shrapnel of about 5.2 in Calibre fired at about 3 or 4 min: intervals; luckily no casualties.	
" "	31 & 31/10		Nothing of any importance to record. Very bad weather, Cold, days sometimes very misty - whole country side a sodden mass - Mud in Trenches and communication Trenches very bad indeed.	skm

31-10-1915.

E A Morris Lieut Colonel RFA
Commanding 80 Bde RFA

"B" 80 Bde RFA

Kindly fill in answers to undermentioned Queries as early as possible and return to me. Use Sheet 6. VOORMEZEELE.

Queries —	
(a) Position of Battery. (b) — " — of forward Gun's (if any) (c) — " — of Anti Air Gun (if any).	~~N 4 d 2.5~~ N 4 d 2.5 — H 35 a 4.4
Position of O.P. No. 1. No. 2.	H 35 d 1.2.
Points between which ground can be seen from respective O.P.	1. O 3 b/d to O 2 c/O 8 a
(1) Describe Zone on which you can bring fire to bear. (2) Give point taken for Zero line in that Zone.	The MOUND to O 2 c 5.1 on Zero line O 2 d 1.7. + all registered points.
Points in enemy's line already registered — giving Range and a.o.s. found —	a.s. Range O 4 c 8.0 +10' 5450 (aeroplane) O 15 d 9.9 +5' 5300 (aeroplane) O 8 b 6.5 +5' 3900 (Night firing) O 13 a 4.8 +10' 2800 O 18 b 4.9 +5' 2350 O 3 d 4.2 +15' 4600 O 2 c 7.5 +5' 3550 O 2 d 0.6 +5' 3675 O 2 d 1.7 +5' 3750

A copy of above to be kept and any change, such as new O.P. or new register to be reported —

HMorgan Lt HdQrs 80

CONFIDENTIAL.

The Officer i/c.
Adjutant's General's
Office
Base

"C"

8o. 15ye R.fa

Kindly fill in answers to undermentioned Queries as early as possible and return to me. Use Sheet VOORMEZEELE

Queries:	
(a) Position of Battery.	N 4 a 17
(b) " " of forward Guns (if any)	—
(c) " " of Anti A/c Guns (if any)	—
Position of O.P.	
No 1.	N 5 c 54
No 2.	H 36 c 86 selected but not wired up yet
Points between which ground can be seen from respective O.P.s	No 1. From point 26 in N 9 b 6 to point 55 in O 7 c. No 2. From point 28 Piccadilly farm to point 28 north of the mound
(1) Describe Zone on which you can bring fire to bear. (2) Give point taken for Zero line in that Zone.	1. On the zone stated above 2. 1. Three trees on edge of Grand Bois marked by point 48. 2. Piccadilly farm
Points on enemy's line already registered - giving Range and A.S. found.	Three trees point 48. A S + 20 mts R. 2950 Wood behind Hollantsfarm AS+20mts R.2850 Piccadilly farm A S + 5 mts R. 3500 Eickopp farm AS +20 R 4800

A copy of above to be kept and any change, such as new O.P. or new register to be reported.

Amongst H.Q's

D/80 Bde R.F.a.

Kindly fill in answers to undermentioned Queries as early as possible and return to me. Use Sheet 6 VOORMEZEELE

Queries —

(a) Position of Battery.	(a). H 29 d 3.6.
(b) " " of forward Guns (if any)	(b) N 6 b 3. 8
(c) " " of Anti Air Gun (if any)	Nil
Position of O.P. Nº 1. Nº 2.	Nº 1. H 35 d 6.4. Nil
Points between which ground can be seen from respective O.P.	The MOUND O 2 d. to S end of Squares O 2 c & d.
(1) Describe Zone on which you can bring fire to bear. (2) Gun point taken for Zero line in that Zone.	(1). As above. enemy's fire or Communication trenches. (2) The MOUND
Points in enemy's line already registered — giving Range and A.o.S. found —	The MOUND — 4300ˣ A)S 30' + EIKHOF FM. 4500 A)S. 30' +

A Copy of above to be kept and any change, such a new O.P. or new register to be reported —

17th K wream

So E/Sec: RPa.
Vol 5
121/7624

Nov 15

WAR DIARY or INTELLIGENCE SUMMARY

Army Form C. 2118

Lieut + Adjt Morgan R.F.A.
50 Brigade R.F.A.
17 Division
2nd New Army.

Place	Date	Hour	Summary of Events and Information	Remarks and references to Appendices
ZILLEBEKE ETg N.G. I.15a 1.1.	1st /11/15		Reference map Sheet 28 Last 1/20000 +1/10000 BELGIUM. Still very wet weather. Enemy Artillery very active. Great difficulty experienced in registering guns of 3rd Div. R.A. which so made look out. They were in such a bad condition that O.C. Bde protested.	
— " —	4/11/15	6 pm to 7 pm	Enemy Arty opened very heavy fire on Batteries under walls of YPRES firing a great many 5.9 H.E. mixed with Shrapnel. A shell struck the Telephone Dug out of D/50. and it fell in on occupants. Lt. M.W. AULTON SMITH. and four Telephonists killed. Also eight men wounded.	
— " —	5/11/15	6·30 pm to 7·30 pm	Enemy shells the vicinity of Bde H.Q. I.15 d.1.1. sending over about 200 shells from direction of Hill 60. No casualties, but much trouble over cut Telephone wires.	
— " —	6/11/15	5 am to 7·30 am	Enemy opened fire on track positions and gun line, a tremendous bombardment, their ammunition very bad, quite 30% of their shells being blinds. All our own guns retaliated. About 6 am, after about one hour with both sides firing heavily, enemy were silenced. Received orders during the day to say allowance of 1gun Ammunition no longer limited, tho' cheered everyone up. Have established unnecessary to be doubled information when	

WAR DIARY
or
INTELLIGENCE SUMMARY

Army Form C. 2118

Frank Morgan Rfa.
80th Brigade R.F.A.
17 Division
2nd Army

Place	Date	Hour	Summary of Events and Information	Remarks and references to Appendices
I.15d.1.1	7/11/15	—	Reference Sheet 28 Scale 1/20000 & 1/10000 Belgium - Capt R.R.W. BELL who went to Hospital on 24/10/75 struck off the strength on being invalided to ENGLAND. 2Lt L. PATTESON joined the Brigade and is posted to D/80. 5th Capt. BUCHAN is posted to the Bde from MEERUT DIVISION joined on 7/11/15. 2Lt M.W. Aulton Smith was posted at H.12.C.9.4. Sheet 28 N.W. just West of YPRES.	hm
-"-	9/11/15	2 pm to 6 pm	Very heavily shelled by all orges of shell, from Field Gun Shrapnel to 8 inch High Explosive. One casualty in B/80. The YPRES SALIENT is a most uncomfortable and difficult place to hold - Guns can fire on our position from almost every direction and certainly from North, East, and South.	hm
-"-	11/11/15	3.45 am.	Warned by 50th Infantry Brigade, that they had received a message from G.H.Q. saying German attack on 11th warned all units, everything ready. No attack came, but enemy bombarded the vicinity of YPRES and ZILLEBEKE from about 10 am to 5 pm. obtained three direct hits on dug-out of B/80, who suffered 5 casualties, wounded, one dial sight put out of action and one Traversing lever damaged. YPRES Cathedral Tower suffered considerably and a goodly number of 17 inch shell fell in the Square	hm

Army Form C. 2118

WAR DIARY
or
INTELLIGENCE SUMMARY
(Erase heading not required.)

Lieut¹ Adjt. Ameau

80th The R Fas
17th Division
2nd New Army

Instructions regarding War Diaries and Intelligence Summaries are contained in F.S. Regs., Part II. and the Staff Manual respectively. Title Pages will be prepared in manuscript.

Place	Date	Hour	Summary of Events and Information	Remarks and references to Appendices
ZILLEBEKE ETANG. I.16.d.1.1.	17/11/1915		Ref. Map. Sheet 28 Scale 1/20,000 & 1/10,000 BELGIUM. The usual shelling (early ducts principally) every day. On 15th inst. H.A. Reserve opened fire on enemy dumps and H.Q at 6pm — Right Group was ordered to co-operate should the enemy retaliate. A signal, 3 red rockets to be fired from H.24. as an order to begin. The rockets were sent up about 5-45pm and each gun fired about 10 rounds each, as rapidly as possible, on enemy communication and support trenches, also searching and sweeping various roads in their area — Bombardment continued about an hour, and it would seem to have been successful as the enemy were extraordinarily quiet all day on 16th — 2/Lieut: H. DENHAM-SMITH joined the Brigade and is posted to A/80, from 5 Reserve Brigade England — Notification received from War Office, Capt. H.CAYLEY, WEBSTER. admitted to Hospital in LONDON, and to be struck off the Strength —	Afm Afm Afm
	19/11/15		Tremendous shelling all day. German fire very effective. Second Lieut: H.W. STRANGMAN. wounded — Two men wounded and one killed in B/80. Several Dug-outs received direct hits —	Afm
	24/11/15			

Army Form C. 2118

WAR DIARY
or
INTELLIGENCE SUMMARY

80 Bde R.F.A.
17 Division
2nd New Army

(Erase heading not required.)

Lieut H Moran. Adjutant.

Instructions regarding War Diaries and Intelligence Summaries are contained in F. S. Regs., Part II. and the Staff Manual respectively. Title Pages will be prepared in manuscript.

Place	Date	Hour	Summary of Events and Information	Remarks and references to Appendices
ZILLE-BEKE ETMNG. ISTOLII.			Reference Map Sheet 28. N.W. T.W. Scale 1/10000 & 1/20000 BELGIUM.	
	24/11/15		Second Lieut: W.T. PARRINGTON. posted to Bde from N°3. Reserve Brigade England — 22-11-15	Atm
	25/11/15		Second Lieut: F.J. SIMMS posted to Bde from N° 5 A Reserve Bde: England — 23-11-15.	Atm
	26/11/15	10 am to 12.30pm	B/60 and Bde H.Q." again shelled, with 5.9 High Explosive from direction of Hill 60. Heavy Arty Reserve noted to him on their fire, and enemy shelling ceased shortly after, 1 wounded in B/60.	Atm

30/11/15.

G H Hughes Lt Colonel R.F.A.
Commanding 80 Bde R.F.A.

60.ᵗᵉ Bde: R.F.A.
Vol: 6
121/7931

WAR DIARY
or
INTELLIGENCE SUMMARY

(Erase heading not required.)

Army Form C. 2118

80th Bde R.F.A.
17th Division
2nd Army

Instructions regarding War Diaries and Intelligence Summaries are contained in F.S. Regs, Part II. and the Staff Manual respectively. Title Pages will be prepared in manuscript.

Place	Date	Hour	Summary of Events and Information	Remarks and references to Appendices
ZILLEBEKE ETANG I.15.d.11	5-12-15		Reference Map Sheet 28 1/10,000 YPRES HOOGE 1/10,000 Lieut R.A. DOBB took over the Adjuncy of the Brigade vice LIEUT. H. MORGAN posted to command 80th Bde Col.	
	8-12-15 Arnt 12-15-15		Hostile artillery more active than during the previous.	
	13-12-15 14-12-15		Very quiet days.	
	9-12-15		Enemy started a [?] attack on the Corps Front in our left, about 5:00 a.m. Heavily bombarded him Section with Gas-Shells & other Shells of all Calibres at the same time. A few fell in the Brigade who received it in the Gas. All Batteries had Shrapnel-helmets and every battery has it use etc. except A/80. The enemy's fire continued the whole day following night a few more Gas-Shells being sent over during to evening. The next day, the 20th and following days more quiet.	
	11.12.15		2nd LIEUT. C.J. LLOYD was posted to the Bde, and was attached to A/80.	R.F.A.
	16.12.15 16.12.15		CAPT. G.F.K. MARSHALL was posted in command of A/D/80, from 79th Bde R.F.A. CAPT. D.A. BUCHAN was posted as a D.A. Divisional Artillery.	R.F.A
	16.12.15		CAPT. F.B. BENHAM from 3rd Divisional Artillery was posted in command of D/80; CAPT. G.F.K. MARSHALL returned to 79th Bde R.F.A.	
	27.12.15		One Section of B/80 came into action for the night in square I.15.b.22	

Army Form C. 2118

WAR DIARY
or
INTELLIGENCE SUMMARY
(Erase heading not required.)

Instructions regarding War Diaries and Intelligence Summaries are contained in F. S. Regs., Part II. and the Staff Manual respectively. Title Pages will be prepared in manuscript.

Place	Date	Hour	Summary of Events and Information	Remarks and references to Appendices
ZILLEBEKE ETANG I.5.d.I.I	28.12.15 A9.12.15		D/80 went out of action last night. During this day, 28.12.15, the enemy fired about 12 17 m. shells into the neighbourhood of LILLE GATE, reserve is there failed to detonate properly.	
	30.12.15	4.30 p.m.	The enemy used gas shells again, forming a barrage very rapidly from about I.14.d.3.4. to I.14.b.5.4.	

E.R. Jackson

So. to Bde. R.F.A.
Vol: 7
Jan '16

01/16

80th Bde. R.F.A.
17th Division
II Army

Army Form C. 2118

WAR DIARY
or
INTELLIGENCE SUMMARY
(Erase heading not required.)

Instructions regarding War Diaries and Intelligence Summaries are contained in F. S. Regs., Part II. and the Staff Manual respectively. Title Pages will be prepared in manuscript.

Place	Date	Hour	Summary of Events and Information	Remarks and references to Appendices
ZILLEBEKE ETANG I.15.a.11	1.1.16		Reference Map: Sheet 28 N.W. 1/10,000 HOOGE. Sheet 27. A quiet day, except for a few gun shells fired by the enemy directed against the vicinity of the LILLE GATE. Orders were received that the Division would shortly go into Rest Billets.	
	2.1.16	6.30 a.m.	Enemy trenches in this Sector were bombarded by the Heavy Artillery and Trench Mortars. No retaliation for this by the enemy.	
	3.1.16	6 a.m.	A hostile Bombing attack against C.3 and adjoining trenches. Batteries immediately ordered to open fire; altogether about 400 rounds were fired. Communication with Front-Line trenches was lost for about 10 min. Considerable amount of hostile shelling all day in this Sector, including a number of gas-shells.	
	4.1.16		GORDON FARM, in which is a battery's O.P., and the other Batteries' O.P's were shelled to-day with 5.9 H.E. O.Return R.Rudge Lt.	

1875 Wt. W593/326 1,000,000 4/15 J.B.C. & A. A.D.S.S./Forms/C.2/18.

WAR DIARY
or
INTELLIGENCE SUMMARY

80th Bde. R.F.A.
17th Division
II Army

Army Form C. 2118

Place	Date	Hour	Summary of Events and Information	Remarks and references to Appendices
ZILLEBEKE ETANG IIS.a.11	3.1.16		Reference Map; Sheet 28 N.W. 1/10,000 HOOGE HAZEBROUCK 9.A. Sheet 27	
			Occasional shelling by the enemy, but, on the whole, three days were quiet.	
	3.1.16		D/80, which was in reserve, marched back to Rest Billets. This night the Battery was billeted at ARNEKE. It proceeded to BONNINGUES, the Rest Billets, the next day.	
			One Section from the Wagon-Lines of A/80, C/80 marched out this day and proceeded to STEENVOORDE, where the guns of one section of A/108, D/108 (24th Division Artillery) were taken over. These sections then proceeded to ARNEKE and billeted there for the night.	
	10.1.16		Both Sections of B/80 marched out (one section linking up with) and proceeded to STEENVOORDE where one section (guns) of B/108 were taken over. B/80 then proceeded to ARNEKE and billeted there for the night.	The two Sections Ammunition Columns were relieved by Ammunition 20/3/16
	10/1/16		Gun detachments of one Section of A/80 and C/80 were relieved this night, by detachments of A/108 and D/108 Retired guns detachments were taken to Billets at ARNEKE, by Motor-Buses.	RB/165

WAR DIARY
INTELLIGENCE SUMMARY
(Erase heading not required.)

80th Bde. R.F.A.
17th Division
II Army.

Army Form C. 2118

Place	Date	Hour	Summary of Events and Information	Remarks and references to Appendices
ZILLEBEKE ETANG IN All	10.1.16		Reference Maps Sheet 18 N.W. 1/10,000 HOOGE. HAZEBROUCK S.A. Sheet 27. The 80th Bde. Am. Col., being relieved by the 108th Bde Am Col., marched out from Lines and proceeded to ARNEKE and billeted there for the night. The Sections of A/80 and C/80, on they marched out of Wagon-Lines, were relieved by Sections of A/108 and D/108 respectively.	
	10.1.16		Remaining Sections of A/80 and C/80, catching the gun horses in by the Sections of A/108 and D/108 respectively, the day before, marched out from Wagon-Lines and proceeded to ARNEKE, and billeted there for the night. The Sections of A/80 and C/80 were relieved by Sections of A/108 and D/108 respectively.	
	11/1/16	6.30 P.m.	Remaining Gun-detachments of A/80 and C/80 relieved by Gun-detachments of A/108 and D/108 respectively. Bde. H.Q. relieved by 108th Bde. H.Q. Relief complete at 6.30 P.m. Whole Relief of 80th Bde. carried out without casualties.	

50th Bde R.F.A.
13th Division
T Army

WAR DIARY
or
INTELLIGENCE SUMMARY

Army Form C. 2118

(Erase heading not required.)

Place	Date	Hour	Summary of Events and Information	Remarks and references to Appendices
HAZEBROUCK			Reference Maps HAZEBROUCK J.A.	
	12.1.16		Retired from detachment of A/50 and B/50 and to Bde. proceeded KARNEKE by Motor Buses, and were billeted to the night. The Units of the Brigade proceeded independently to their billets	
BONNINGUES			at BONNINGUES.	
	13th & 14th		Then period was spent in a general clean-up, and in overhauling equipment & stores.	
	16th		2nd Lieut. W. E. KING was attached to the Brigade and was attached to "A" Battery	
	17th		2nd Lieut. H.D. MARSH was attached to the Brigade and was attached to the Bde. Amm. Col. Marching - Order Route March, Signalling and Horse Drill were carried out during this period	
	20th & 26th			
	23rd		2nd Lieut. H.J. BARTLET was attached to the Brigade and was attached to "B" Battery	
	27th & 31st		The above Course of Training was continued.	

P.H. Freeling
Major R.G.A.
for Lt. Col. R.G.A.
Comdg 50th Bde R.F.A.

80th Brigade R.F.A.
17th Division
II Army

WAR DIARY
or
INTELLIGENCE SUMMARY

Army Form C. 2118

(Erase heading not required.)

Place	Date	Hour	Summary of Events and Information	Remarks and references to Appendices
BONNINGUES	Feb.1st 1916 – Feb. 5th		Ref. Map HAZEBROUCK S.A.100,000. ST. OMER 4. BELGIUM SHEET 28 N.W. Course of Training, as in January, was continued.	
	Feb. 5th		First orders received that the Division would shortly relieve the 3rd Division on the 5th Corps front.	
	Feb. 8th		The Brigade marched to BUYSSCHEURE, and billeted there night 8/9th.	
	Feb. 9th		One officer from each battery went forward to join its Battery of the 42nd Brigade R.F.A. 3rd Division, which his own battery was relieving.	
	Feb. 10th		The Brigade marched to STEENVOORDE, and billeted night 9th/10th on the WATOU ROAD East of STEENVOORDE. 1st Section of Batteries marched to respective Batteries Wagon-Lines of 42nd Bde., which they were relieving, and detachments relieved detachments of 42nd Bde.; 1st Section to gun-line this night. 1st Section Guns handed over to 42nd Bde. at STEENVOORDE. 2nd Section Guns were taken up by 1st Section and handed over to respective W/lines of 42nd Bde.; Non-aiming Section of Batteries and Bde. Ord. Col. marched to respective W/lines of 42nd Bde., and relieved same.	
	Feb. 11th	9.0 a.m.		

Army Form C. 2118

WAR DIARY
or
INTELLIGENCE SUMMARY
(Erase heading not required.)

Ref. (Maps) BELGIUM Sheet 28 N.W.
TRENCH MAPS YOORMEZEELE 1/5000 HALLEBEKE 1/10,000

Place	Date	Hour	Summary of Events and Information	Remarks and references to Appendices
DIEKEBUSCH Night 14th/15th	14th		80th Bde H.Q. relieved 42nd Bde 7.00pm. 2nd Bde Battn. relieved 42nd Bde Battn. Detachments relieved respectively 42nd Bde Battns detachments at same time. Relief complete at 6.30 a.m. when O.C. 80th Bde took over. CENTRE GROUP. Details of Relief with Battery positions: 80th Bde. H.Q. relieved 42nd Bde H.Q. at H 2 d 6.8 A/80 relieved 4.5.A Bty. 42nd Bde at N 4 b 4.4 B/80 relieved 41st Bty. 42nd Bde at H 35 b 4.7 C/80 relieved 29th Bty. 42nd Bde at H 29 d 9.3 D/80 relieved 6th Bty (Scotch) 42nd Bde at H 30 a 2.7 C/81 relieved 130 How. Bty. at H 35 a 7.7 The above to be command of O.C. CENTRE GROUP. CENTRE GROUP covers the zone CANAL (inclusive) S 02 a 7.6 Bombardment of Support Trenches, covered by CENTRE GROUP. All Batteries retaliate as being called upon.	
		4.30 a.m.		
		5.30 p.m. (about)	Enemy dropping a mine opposite NEW YEAR TRENCH on our left.	
		5.45 p.m.	Enemy bombardment into our lines. O.C. CENTRE GROUP ordered all Batteries all fire on B'zaville & Fort in enemy front line trenches	

WAR DIARY
or
INTELLIGENCE SUMMARY

Army Form C. 2118

(Erase heading not required.)

Instructions regarding War Diaries and Intelligence Summaries are contained in F.S. Regs., Part II. and the Staff Manual respectively. Title Pages will be prepared in manuscript.

Ref. Maps. TRENCH MAPS VOORMEZEELE HOLLEBEKE

Place	Date	Hour	Summary of Events and Information	Remarks and references to Appendices
DICKEBUSCH	14.4.15	5.45 A.M.	In this run from O/S1 were ordered to fire in enemy support trenches S. of ST. ELOI. During early part of the morning the enemy occupied NEW YEAR TRENCH.	
		11.30 A.M.	Counter-attack delivered by 82 J. INF. BDE. CENTRE GROUP formed a barrage around eastern edge of the CRATER of this mine, and across enemy support trenches opposite NEW YEAR TRENCH. The Objective was not gained in the counter-attack.	
	15.4	4.30 A.M.	The Counter-attack was re-delivered with the same support by CENTRE GROUP. The attack did not gain its objective. By this time the situation had become that the enemy occupied NEW YEAR TRENCH, and the eastern end of the BLUFF.	
	15.4	9 A.M.	O.P. was reported that the enemy had a machine-gun on the BLUFF.	
		9.30 A.M.	O.C. C/81 was ordered to fire on this. The BLUFF was fired into more of the day, by battalion of the CENTRE GROUP.	
		9 P.M.	A counter-attack was to be delivered on the BLUFF. The actual attack by the CENTRE GROUP was as follows:-	

WAR DIARY
or
INTELLIGENCE SUMMARY

(Erase heading not required.)

Army Form C. 2118

Instructions regarding War Diaries and Intelligence Summaries are contained in F. S. Regs., Part II. and the Staff Manual respectively. Title Pages will be prepared in manuscript.

Regt. Maps.

TRENCH MAPS VOORMEZEELE HOLLEBEKE 10,000

Place	Date	Hour	Summary of Events and Information	Remarks and references to Appendices
DICKEBUSCH			1. On hostile barrage along the enemy front line from the CANAL through I.34.d. by B/180. This was kept up by B/180 from 8.30 p.m. until 9.30 a.m. for 16th inst. Reports received that carriage should be kept up on our front.	
			2. Army Commanders and Support trenches in the area 0.4.6.3.— 0.4.6.4.b – I.34.d.01 were reached by D/180 and C/61 from 8.0 a.m. to 9.15 a.m.	
	9th		It was reported by 52nd INF. BDE. that the BLUFF was with a enemy hands, & an counter-attack had been postponed and that it would take place at 11.30 a.m. This was also was taken by the CENTRE GROUP. The reply was however that till 3.35 a.m. the line at the BLUFF at a slow rate of fire	
	Nov 15-16 M17pm	B/180 and C/89 were firing continuously on the BLUFF at a slow rate of fire from 8.30 p.m. to 6.0 a.m. From 5.0 a.m. to 5.35 a.m. this rate of fire was considerably increased so as to make a regiment to embark. The latter was to commence with the SOS signal also sweeping the	
	16th 11.45 pm	4.30 a.m. – 5.30 a.m. Army reported that a few S.O.H.E. – sweeping of D/80's position. The East most line of a day-art of the battery supporting the gallery.	

(all A D/80)

WAR DIARY or INTELLIGENCE SUMMARY

Army Form C. 2118

Ref- MAP - TRENCH MAPS VOORMEZEELE 1/5000 + HOLLEBEKE 1/10,000

Place	Date	Hour	Summary of Events and Information	Remarks and references to Appendices
DICKEBUSH				
	17th	6.a-	No. 534.5.3 Sergt. HOLLANDS W.J. (since died of wounds) No. 52926 Cpl. TINDALL C.W. No. 1660 Gnr. SIMONS A.W. 2/Lt W.E. KING B/90 was wounded at Battalion H.Q. at SPOIL BANK. B/90 and C/89 firing all day on the BLUFF at a slow rate of fire. allfiredly.	
	Night 17th/18th		B/90 and C/89 firing all night on the BLUFF at a slow rate of fire; the Tunnel running from points 5.7 – 7½ s., O4a was also shelled intermittently during the night.	
	Night 18th/19th		B/90 and C/89 firing on BLUFF and trench running from point 5.7 – 7½ s., O4a on enemy working parties on the BLUFF. Enem. Mor. Rom. B/90, C/90 and O/87 firing on the BLUFF.	
	19th 2.P.m.		O/87 shelled trenches about ST. ELOI. Divisional Artillery Retaliation "B" and "E" ordered.	
	about 2.0 p.		5.9 H.E. Shell fell near D/90. No. 28366 Gr. MORGAN J.H. C/90 wounded by splinter from one A.A. shell.	
	20th			

WAR DIARY or INTELLIGENCE SUMMARY

Army Form C. 2118

Trench Map: YPRES
Ref. Map: YOORNEZEELE 10/100 POPERINGHE 10/100

Place	Date	Hour	Summary of Events and Information	Remarks and references to Appendices
DICKEBUSCH	20th		A fairly quiet day. Enemy signalled by aeroplane towards position 0.3.a.9.2. when 5.9 H.E. and a few 8.2. on the last ten minutes hostile aeroplane were active. During this night they were signally to their infantry with red, white, and blue lights.	
	21st	5.0 p.m.	Enemy bombarded front-line and support trenches to left. Battalion B/80 and D/80 retaliated, and enemy fire ceased.	
	22nd		Quiet day.	
	23rd	3.45 p.m. – 4.50 p.m.	Enemy put 5.9"s in and about SUICIDE COPSE.	
		7.30 p.m.	A few more in same neighbourhood.	
		4.30 – 4.35 p.m.	B/80 and C/81 fired 25 rounds in zone O.4.a.30 – 6 – 9.1. Then in conjunction with 14 Hoars Arty.	
		4.30 – 4.55 p.m.		
	24th		All quiet. C/81 firing slow on A. BLUFF.	

WAR DIARY
or
INTELLIGENCE SUMMARY

(Erase heading not required.)

Ref. Map — Trench Maps — VOORMEZEELE 10,000 HOLLEBEKE 10,000

Place	Date	Hour	Summary of Events and Information	Remarks and references to Appendices
DICKEBUSCH	26th	3·55 p.m.	Divisional Reliefs "C" ordered. Enemy made a bombardment attack on Trenches 32+, 33g, 34, held by 52nd INF. BDE. Communication with those trenches was broken, but it was apparent that 52nd Bde was considerably shaken, with Troops Making INF reported that enemy were Shelling front of one of ME Trenches in rear of CENTRE GROUP. All batteries immediately retaliated on enemy C.M.E. Trenches. B/80 (2 guns) and C/81 fired up in front of 52 & 53 INF. BDE. A/80 Art Communication with 53 Infantry, and formed a barrage butt over enemy trenches until communication was restored.	
	29th	3·0 p.m.	Hostile batteries opened fire with 5·15 Howitzers & 9·2 Bns. in position about #12 q A 35	
		3·30 p.m.	About 12 gas-shells were fired at the same position, very rapidly. C/81 fired firing against the BLUFF at a slow rate of fire.	

[signed] Lt-Col R.F.A.
Cmdg. 80th Bde R.F.A.

WAR DIARY
—or—
INTELLIGENCE SUMMARY

(Erase heading not required.)

Ref. Maps:—

Army Form C. 2118

80th Brigade R.F.A.
17a Division
II Army

Place	Date	Hour	Summary of Events and Information	Remarks and references to Appendices
DICKEBUSCH			Trench Maps VOORMEZEELE 28 S.W. HOOGE BEKE 28 N.W.	
	1.3.16	5.00am	Preparation for the counter-attack on the BLUFF this morning, which were occupied by the enemy was heavily shelled up by a severe bombardment. All three CENTRE GROUP had men in the trench to his support, one battery allotted to the 3rd Inf.Bde. The bombardment was heavy & continued till 3/4 hour.	
	2.3.16	4.30am	The BLUFF and heights to the East above were gained by the infantry at 4.30 am. At 4.32 am a general bombardment of the whole of the enemy's entrenchments. The men kept up a steady rate of fire, which was replied to by a counter at a steady rate. By 10.30 am the state of affairs had become very quiet, and batteries were able to cease firing. Bn. Hq NORFOLK ROAD, C/80 relieved C Army OME howitzers remained S. of CANAL.	

WAR DIARY or INTELLIGENCE SUMMARY

Army Form C. 2118

(Erase heading not required.)

Place	Date	Hour	Summary of Events and Information	Remarks and references to Appendices
DICKEBUSCH			Trench Maps:- VOORMEZEELE 28 S.W. 1. 10,000	
	2.3.16	4 P.M.	Trench 28 heavily shelled. Immediate retaliation carried out by B/80 (our covering battery) and C/81.	
N9 2/3			VOORMEZEELE heavily shelled. One battery of LEFT GROUP was out of action, and unable to co-operate Trench 2.9. O.C. CENTRE GROUP switched D/80 to cover this Trench. Trench 28 shelled about continuously the whole day at B/80 constantly firing over this Trench, in retaliation.	
	3.3.16	4.30 a.m.	Shelling of Trench 28 became very heavy. B/80 and C/81 retaliated with heavy shelling of trenches opposite 28.	
		5.15 A.M.	SPOIL BANK shelled by enemy. B/80 and C/81 switched to very slow fire to leave a margin to shoot immediately S.O.S. CANAL. The situation became quiet by about 6.0 a.m.	

1875 Wt. W593/826 1,000,000 4/15 J.B.C. & A. A.D.S.S./Forms/C. 2118.

Army Form C. 2118

WAR DIARY
or
INTELLIGENCE SUMMARY

(Erase heading not required.)

Reg. No. ...

BC 4 Brigade R.F.A.
V Corps
Second Army

Place	Date	Hour	Summary of Events and Information	Remarks and references to Appendices
DICKEBUSCH	18/11		Trench Map VOORMEZEELE 1/10,000 HILL 60 1/5000 BLAZEKRUISE 1/10000 Relief of 80th Bde. by 42nd Bde. during the night. First Section of A, B, C, and D/80 were relieved by First Sections of Relieving Batteries of 42nd Bde. First Section of each Battery were relieved by 2nd Major Lines during the day. Relief completed by 7.30 p.m. Remaining Sections of Batteries relieved during the night. Also group Hdqrs. Remount Station & Major Lines relieved during the day. Bde. Am. Col. relieved during the day by 4-2nd Bde. Am. Col. Relief completed by 8.15 p.m. All units marched to Rest Billets — Areas, HdQ 2nd Cross Roads N. of B — BORRE — LE BRIARDE — LE BRUL ROAD	

Army Form C. 2118

WAR DIARY
or
INTELLIGENCE SUMMARY
(Erase heading not required.)

Instructions regarding War Diaries and Intelligence Summaries are contained in F.S. Regs., Part II. and the Staff Manual respectively. Title Pages will be prepared in manuscript.

R.F.A. Major HAZEBROUCK SA Sheets 36, 3GA

Place	Date	Hour	Summary of Events and Information	Remarks and references to Appendices
LE KREUL	12–17 March		These days were spent in a general clean-up, and new kind of equipment. Orders were received that 17th Division would relieve 21st Division on II Corps Front.	
	18th		80th Brigade R.F.A. to relieve 96th Bde. R.F.A. of the 21st Div. 1st Section A/80 ↔ B/80 marched up this day and relieved First Section A/96 ↔ B/96 respectively. Relieved Gun detachment as the first took place during the night.	
	19th		2nd Section A/80 ↔ B/80 marched up and relieved 2nd Section of A/96 ↔ B/96 respectively. 80th Bde. Amm. Col. marched up and relieved 96th Bde. Amm. Col.	
	20th		1st Section C/D/80 marched and relieved 1st Section C/96 ↔ D/96 respectively.	
	21st		2nd Section C/D/80 marched out and relieved 2nd Section C/96 ↔ D/96 respectively.	

WAR DIARY
or
INTELLIGENCE SUMMARY

Army Form C. 2118

(Erase heading not required.)

Ref Map 36 36A TRENCH MAP WEZ MACQUART

Place	Date	Hour	Summary of Events and Information	Remarks and references to Appendices
ARMENTIERES	23rd		80th Bde H.Q. relieved 96th Bde H.Q.	
	"	12 noon	O.C. 80th Bde. assumed command of RIGHT GROUP consisting of in our brigade area D/81 (How.)	
	24th – 31st		On the whole the period has been quiet, with a very few exceptions: e.g.	
	26th	3.30 pm	5th Inf. Bde reported that our Artillery line had been shelled by the enemy most of the day. A, C, D/80 retaliated on important points behind enemy lines.	
			Enemy shells railway crossing at I.2.a.10, D/80 retaliation on ARRET I.12.c.10.8	
	29th noon		Most of these days there has been a hostile "airplane" over sending over occasional rounds in vicinity I.22.0.2	
	31st		of CHAPELLE D'ARMENTIÈRES 6 Officers and 90 O.R.'s of Australian Artillery were attached to Batteries of the Brigade, for instructional purposes.	

Signed .... Lt-Col R.F.A
Cmdg. 80 RFA Bde R.F.A

Army Form C. 2118

XVII

WAR DIARY
or
INTELLIGENCE SUMMARY
(Erase heading not required.)

Instructions regarding War Diaries and Intelligence Summaries are contained in F.S. Regs, Part II. and the Staff Manual respectively. Title Pages will be prepared in manuscript.

Ref. Map: Sheet 36. 36a. Trench Map WEZ MACQUART 1/10,000 Second Army

[margin annotations: RFA 80th Bde / II Corps / Vol 10]

Place	Date	Hour	Summary of Events and Information	Remarks and references to Appendices
ARMENTIÈRES	12/4/16	From 9.35 am till 12.20 pm	B/80 Gun position I.2.a.8.5. was heavily shelled by 21 cm, 15 cm, 10 cm & 7.7 cm shells; about 200 rounds in all. The shelling was severe, direct hits being obtained on 150 gun pits. The hits were thought to be obtained by 15 cm shells. One howitzer in a gun emplacement which hit on the gun turret, or one of its action. The shield was obtained on a French steel dugout; the shell failed to penetrate, and no damage was done to the gun. Nr 113 instr. ten rounds, watching & bracket, was yesterday unity & presently rejecting it. During the day about 50 7.7cm shells were fired at CROSS ROADS I.2.c.0.2.	
	13th	All day	The enemy shelled B/80's farm with 7.7 cm shells. Two direct hits were obtained on one of 7 rounds that were fired.	
	14th	12 noon		
	16th	3.45 to 4 pm	FARM I.9.a.7.8 again shelled by 7.7 cm shells; about 12 rounds fell; one direct hit was obtained on the building.	
	20th	12 noon (approx)	7.7 cm. Battery fired a few rounds against B/80's Farm (I.9.a.7.8). B/80 immediately retaliated on Hostile Battery, which then ceased firing.	

Army Form C. 2118

2

WAR DIARY
INTELLIGENCE SUMMARY

(Erase heading not required.)

Instructions regarding War Diaries and Intelligence Summaries are contained in F. S. Regs., Part II. and the Staff Manual respectively. Title Pages will be prepared in manuscript. Ref. Maps

Place	Date	Hour	Summary of Events and Information	Remarks and references to Appendices
ARMENTIERES			Trench Map. W E 2 MASQUART. Sheets 36, 36a.	
	20th	3.0 p.m.	D/180, at Infantry request, retaliated a RAILWAY SALIENT and ARRET I1240 (Enemy had the shells Trener 73).	
	21st	11 A.M.	Hostile 4.2 How. Battery immediately opened fire on ASYLUM. No casualties. 5 personnel a equipment. Hostile Battery 7.7 cm fired about 10 rounds at B/180's Farm (I9a78); no casualties.	
		5.0 P.M. (approx)	D/180 then about 8 rounds on enemy trench tramway in vicinity of I12 central.	
	24th	—	Hostile 7.7 cm Battery fired 6 rounds at D/180. All OK. which fell around as gun emplacement.	
	Night 24/25th		3 men slightly wounded; 1 dial sight damaged. D/180 moved 2 guns into new position at C27c19. D/180 registered the 2 guns in the new position.	
	25th		6 7.7 cm. about 100 yds short of Gun in [?]. Store [?] fine.	

1875 Wt. W593/826 1,000,000 4/15 J.B.C. & A. A.D.S.S./Forms/C. 2118.

Army Form C. 2118

WAR DIARY
or
INTELLIGENCE SUMMARY

(Erase heading not required.)

Instructions regarding War Diaries and Intelligence Summaries are contained in F. S. Regs., Part II. and the Staff Manual respectively. Title Pages will be prepared in manuscript.

Ref. Map Trench Map 1/10,000 WEZ MACQUART

Place	Date	Hour	Summary of Events and Information	Remarks and references to Appendices
ARMENTIERES			Sheets 36, 36a	3
	25th			
	26th	3 p.m.	Hostile shelling in vicinity of D/187. D/181 fires in conjunction with the General shoot by Left Group. B/180 & D/181 retaliated on Hostile Battery at 37 a 16, reported active by Aeroplane. Hostile Battery fired about 30 Heavy Shrapnel about new position of D/180's 2 guns. No. 5 & 991 Gun. G. COPAS D/180 wounded & arm.	
	27th	4 p.m.	D/180 fires a few rounds from 4" old position, I2a 6.5. Enemy retaliated on their position with about 30 rounds from a Trench Gun.	
	28th	4.15 p.m. (approx)	A few 4.2 H.E. about I3c, and vicinity of D/187.	

Army Form C. 2118

WAR DIARY
INTELLIGENCE SUMMARY
(Erase heading not required.)

Instructions regarding War Diaries and Intelligence Summaries are contained in F. S. Regs., Part II. and the Staff Manual respectively. Title Pages will be prepared in manuscript.

Ref. Map Sheets 36, 36a. WEZ MACQUART 1:10,000

Place	Date	Hour	Summary of Events and Information	Remarks and references to Appendices
ARMENTIERES	29th	3.15pm	Hostile working parties at ARRET Ixd07, and supposed battery position J13b21 dispersed by our artillery.	
		3.30pm	A few rounds fired J13b21	
			Hostile artillery fairly active. About 4.5, 4.2 H.E. tried into the ASYLUM between 2.0pm. and 3.0pm.	
	30th		A few 7.7 c.m. in vicinity of I1eo2. Quiet day in this sector. Enemy put a few H.E. 4" I3d	

M[signature]
Lt. Col. R.F.A.
O. in C. 80th Bde. R.F.A.

XVII

80th Brigade R.F.A.
17th Division Vol II
Second Army

WAR DIARY
INTELLIGENCE SUMMARY
(Erase heading not required.)

Army Form C. 2118

Instructions regarding War Diaries and Intelligence Summaries are contained in F.S. Regs., Part II. and the Staff Manual respectively. Title Pages will be prepared in manuscript. **Ref. Maps**

Place	Date	Hour	Summary of Events and Information	Remarks and references to Appendices
ARMENTIÈRES	May 1916.		Trench Map WEZ MACQUART 1:10000 Sheet 36, 36a.	
	2nd	8.30 a.m. – 1.30 p.m.	About 35 – 5.9 H.E. fell in the immediate vicinity of D/81. It is thought that there were a few 8″ shells, but it has not been possible to confirm this.	
	3rd	11.30 a.m.	Retaliation on enemy Front-line trenches by A, B, & C/80 at request of Infantry; enemy having been firing on our support trenches.	
		3.0 p.m. approx.	About 12 rounds from S.P. of H.R. directed at Church of SACRÉ COEUR C.26.d.35. this is the O.P. of D/80. Two direct hits were obtained on the Church.	
			A few rounds, thought to be 4.2 H.E. fell about in RUE NATIONALE, ARMENTIÈRES.	
	5th		Enemy working parts. dispersed by B battery. Retaliation by D battery on French 72. A quiet day.	

WAR DIARY
INTELLIGENCE SUMMARY

Army Form C. 2118

Ref Map Sheet 36. 36a.

Place	Date	Hour	Summary of Events and Information	Remarks and references to Appendices
ARMENTIERES	5th	6.30 p.m.	Enemy opened sharp bombardment of Trenches 71, 72, 73. Covering Eastern C & D/80 immediately opened a heavy retaliation. Report was received from 5th INF. BDE. that it was thought that enemy had cleared in from his opposite their trenches. Accordingly C & D/80 were directed to bring the bulk of their fire to bear on Support trenches opposite 71, 72, 73. At the same time D/81 were directed to fire on their same support trenches. The hostile shells slackened, + all became quiet on our front.	Sheet 36, 36a. 1:10,000.
		7 p.m.	Immediately afterwards, a very heavy bombardment was opened by the enemy on the Australian Division front. Gas-alarms were sounded practically all along the line.	

WAR DIARY
INTELLIGENCE SUMMARY
(Erase heading not required.)

Army Form C. 2118

Instructions regarding War Diaries and Intelligence Summaries are contained in F. S. Regs., Part II. and the Staff Manual respectively. Title Pages will be prepared in manuscript.

Ref. Map Sheets 36, 36a

Above Map WE2 MACQUART 1.10,000

Place	Date	Hour	Summary of Events and Information	Remarks and references to Appendices
ARMENTIÈRES	5th	7:15 a.m.	Infantry in our own front reported all quiet. A number of S-shells fell in various parts of the Town about 8 p.m. shells fell in the immediate vicinity of D/80's position; some of these were 5.9. A few 5.9 fell in vicinity of RIGHT GROUP BATTLE HDQRS., I.a.5.½.2.	
		9.30	All quiet.	
	7 A.3. appr.		B/80 fired a hostile battery at J.13a. Hostile shells directed against ST. CHARLES CHURCH and vicinity of A/80.	
	8th		A few 7.7 and 4 CHAPELLE D'ARMENTIÈRES. It has now been arranged that if the enemy shell CHAPELLE D'ARMENTIÈRES we shall retaliate on WEZ MACQUART with at least 1 18 pdr. battery and 1 4.5" How. bty.	

Army Form C. 2118

WAR DIARY
INTELLIGENCE SUMMARY
(Erase heading not required.)

Instructions regarding War Diaries and Intelligence Summaries are contained in F.S. Regs., Part II. and the Staff Manual respectively. Title Pages will be prepared in manuscript.

Place	Date	Hour	Summary of Events and Information	Remarks and references to Appendices
			Ref Maps	
ARMENTIERES			Sheet 36, 36a French Map W E 2 MACQUART 1/10,000.	
	7th		9 Officers and 30 O.R's of N.Z.F.A. attached to the Brigade for duty; and were distributed amongst the Batteries of the Group.	
	9th		Orders received that Brigade Ammunition Columns would be abolished. The D.A.C. to be increased & Supply of Ammunition to come direct from that Unit. CAPT. H. MORGAN from Command, 80 x R.A.C. to command No. 4 Section 17th D.A.C.	
			2/LIEUT. J. C. CURRIE is attached at C/80 from 80th B.A.C.	
			2/LIEUT. H.S. MARSH is attached to A/80 from 80th B.A.C.	
			2/LIEUT. H.J. BARTLET proceeded with details of 80 x B.A.C. to Base, under O.C. 79th B.A.C.	

WAR DIARY
or
INTELLIGENCE SUMMARY

(Erase heading not required.)

Army Form C. 2118

Instructions regarding War Diaries and Intelligence Summaries are contained in F.S. Regs., Part II. and the Staff Manual respectively. Title Pages will be prepared in manuscript. Ref Map.

Place	Date	Hour	Summary of Events and Information Ref Map WE 2 MARCQUART 1/40,000	Remarks and references to Appendices
ARMENTIÈRES	10th – 13th	Sheets 36, 36A.	On the whole very quiet days. A few occasional retaliations on enemy mat- but not request of Infantry.	
	14th	9 AM 12 n	Orders received that the Division would be relieved by the NEW ZEALAND DIVISION. 80th Bde. to be relieved by 2nd N.Z. F.A. 13 on the 17th. The 17th Division to move into Area of ST. OMER for 10 days' intensive training. F.A.B's are going to be reorganised. 80th Bde will consist of A/80, B/80, C/80 and D/81 (how.). This change to take place about May 21st. D/81 will be re-named D/80. D/80 will be transferred to a Bde. 17th Div.	

WAR DIARY or INTELLIGENCE SUMMARY

Army Form C. 2118

(Erase heading not required.)

Ref Maps **Sheet 36, 36a WEZ MACQUART Trench Map** 1:10,000 1:20,000

Place	Date	Hour	Summary of Events and Information	Remarks and references to Appendices
ARMENTIERES	14th	7.0 pm 9.10 pm	D/81 opened fire in enemy front line opposite 69 & 71 C/80 in O.M.E. & Support trenches opposite to MUSHROOM. This was at the request of the Infantry who thought that the enemy might be assembling here for a raid.	
		9.30 pm	The above ceased fire. Slight retaliation by enemy.	
	13/14th		This night the N.Z. Inf. Bde. relieved the 59th Inf. Bde.	
	14th		By 1.0 am all Batteries of the 80th Brigade were relieved by Batteries of 2nd BDE. N.Z.F.A.	
		3.50 am	O.C. 80th BDE. handed over command to O.C. 2nd BDE. N.Z.F.A.	
		10.0 am	The Brigade marched under O.C. Brigade to LA BLEUE and billeted there for the night.	

WAR DIARY
or
INTELLIGENCE SUMMARY

Army Form C. 2118

(Erase heading not required.)

Instructions regarding War Diaries and Intelligence Summaries are contained in F.S. Regs., Part II and the Staff Manual respectively. Title Pages will be prepared in manuscript. Ref. Maps.

Place	Date	Hour	Summary of Events and Information	Remarks and references to Appendices
ARMENTIERES	17"	2.20 a.m.	One Casualty suffered by Brigade today: G.A. MORGAN D/80 killed in action. No. 50986 after rifle-bullet. Whilst reading out about a communication, by strong rifle-bullet, head.	
	18"		Battu. marched independently to RENESCURE, & were billeted there for the night.	
	19"		Brigade marched under O.C. Brigade to Billets - Train Area — ACQUIN.	
ACQUIN	20"		Overhaul of Harness, equipment. General Clean-up. Battery D/80 left the Brigade this day, & was replaced by D/81 (How.)	
	21" 22" }		Battery Drill of all Batteries. A Signallers Class is held each day at BDE HQ for 2 hours. Special attention is being paid to Visual Signals.	

1875 Wt. W593/826 1,000,000 4/15 J.B.C. & A. A.D.S.S./Forms/C. 2118.

Army Form C. 2118

WAR DIARY
INTELLIGENCE SUMMARY
(Erase heading not required.)

Place	Date	Hour	Summary of Events and Information	Remarks and references to Appendices
HAZEBROUCK S.A.				
AcQUIN	23rd		Tactical Scheme under D.C. Brigade	
	26th	8 p.m.	Night Operation. Brigade practised moving up & withdrawing from positions under cover of darkness	
	27th		80th Brigade carried out operations. Divisional Train Area, with attached Infantry Brigade 51st INF BDE. Tactical Scheme in Divisional Train Area under C.O. Brigade. The Chief point of exercise was the occupying of new positions in an advance and carrying out communication by runners.	
	29th & 30th	3.30 p.m. – 9.15 p.m.	Operation under the G.O.C. Division.	
	31st		Batteries at Boston conducted dispersal	
	29th		Operation under the C.R.A.	

W Manders Lt Col R.F.A.
Cmdg. 80th Bde R.F.A.

WAR DIARY
INTELLIGENCE SUMMARY

Army Form C. 2118

80th BDE. R.F.A.
17th Division
Second Army

Ref. Maps.

Place	Date	Hour	Summary of Events and Information	Remarks and references to Appendices
EQUIN	June 1st	9.12 a.m.	HAZEBROUCK S.A. Divisional Artillery Route March. The Brigade afterwards proceeded to the Training Area and carried out Tactical Exercise.	
	3rd		Divisional Operations in Training Area.	
	5th	2.30 p.m.	Under C.R.A's orders, C/80 was detailed to practise a crossing trenches.	
	6th		Operation with 51st. INF. BDE. were to have been carried out this day, but were postponed till following day, owing to heavy rain.	
	7th		These Operations were again suspended owing to bad weather. The Brigade, however, carried out a Tactical Scheme & practice of crossing trenches. Orders were received later for Divisional Artillery would commence to leave the Training Area on night 10th/11th. to March by road.	

WAR DIARY
or
INTELLIGENCE SUMMARY

(Erase heading not required.)

Army Form C. 2118

Instructions regarding War Diaries and Intelligence Summaries are contained in F.S. Regs., Part II. and the Staff Manual respectively. Title Pages will be prepared in manuscript. Ref Map.

Place	Date	Hour	Summary of Events and Information	Remarks and references to Appendices
ACQUIN	10/7/18		HAZEBROUCK S.A. LENS. AMIENS.	
		10/11 pm	This night the Brigade marched to THEROUANNE and billeted there for the night, arriving ACQUIN about 8.30 —	
	11/7/18		This night to ANVIN and billeted there for the night —	
	12/7/18		" " BOCQUE MAISON " "	
	13/7/18		" " VILLERS BOCAGE " "	
	14/7/18		" " HEILLY camped	
			On our three marches the Divisional Artillery was marching as a whole.	
	15/7/18		This afternoon the Brigade marched to BONNAY and camped. The Division is now in the XV Corps, Fourth Army. The 80th Brigade R.F.A. is attached to the 7th Division. The enemy 31st Section of Battery of 7th Divnal Battery. 1st Section of D/80 Battery of 80th F.A.B. relieved. The whole of D/80 turned into action.	
	17/7/18		The enemy 2nd Section A Battery of 80th F.A.B. relieved 3 Section A Battery of 7th Divnal Battery.	

Army Form C. 2118
80. R.F.A.
vol 12

WAR DIARY
or
INTELLIGENCE SUMMARY
XVII
(Erase heading not required.)

Ref. Maps 62 d N.E. TRENCH MAP MONTAUBAN 1:20,000.

Place	Date	Hour	Summary of Events and Information	Remarks and references to Appendices
GIBRALTAR	24.vi.		Orders have now been received to the effect that the FOURTH ARMY will take the Offensive. The days of Preliminary Bombardment are lettered Un., U, V, W, X, Y; and Z day will be the day of assault; hour of assault to be Zero hour, which will be Infantry's date.	
	25.vi.		U day is the 24th June. Up to this day inclusive batteries are registering on the combatted the	
	26.vi. 28.vi.		The targets given to batteries of this Brigade consist of seven of the enemy's trenches, M. G. emplacements, O.P.'s, & Shell Points. At night batteries are to keep up steady rate of fire to prevent enemy repairing his wire.	

E J Jackson Lt-Col. R.F.A.
Cmdg. 80th Bde. R.F.A.

17th Div.
XV.Corps.

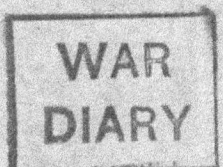

Headquarters,

80th BRIGADE, R.F.A.

J U L Y
(29.6.16 - 31.7.16)
1 9 1 6

WAR DIARY
or
INTELLIGENCE SUMMARY

(Erase heading not required.)

Army Form C. 2118

Ref maps.

Place	Date	Hour	Summary of Events and Information	Remarks and references to Appendices
GIBRALTER			62 D.N.E. TRENCH MAP MONTAUBAN 1:20000	
	29/6/16		Premature occurred in D battery causing eight casualties including 2 Nos 1.	later
	30/6/16		The expenditure of ammunition during preceding week to the Bn was #6540A. 3690 AX.	
	1/7/16			
	8/7/16		The Bde moved from its position in HAPPY VALLEY and took up its position at CARNOY. 9 of Casualties in the Bde since the 1st Ammunition to 1 killed 99 wounded. Amount of Ammunition expended since the beginning of the bomb operation 5/6/16 E total. 24437 AX. Very heavy rain interupts all work trays telephone & walk cars damaged by shelling. In Expenditure of Ammunition since 14/7/16 was	
CARNOY MAP REF. 7/7/16 AM15 M517 I.J.	8/7/16 12/7/16 14/7/16		14050A. and 7920 AX The number of Casualties which took place during this week was 2 killed and 22 wounded.	total
		3.25 A.M.	1st attack on BAZENTINLE GRANDE took place	

WAR DIARY or INTELLIGENCE SUMMARY

Army Form C. 2118

Place	Date	Hour	Summary of Events and Information	Remarks and references to Appendices
REF MAP LONGUEVAL 22 a.5.	15/7/16		French Map MONTAUBAN LONGUEVAL 1:20,000 In the Evening the Bde moved from CARNOY to the Ridge N.E. of MONTAUBAN, in Bde position the Battn. were subjected to very heavy shelling by the enemy.	
	18/7/16		In the morning Major M.J.K. O'MALLEY-KEYES was wounded whilst on duty as forward observing officer, and during the afternoon Major P.H. PRESTON was wounded at his Battery position. The former was commanding A battery and the latter B battery. Capt Cannan assumed C batg war wounded and the remains of A batg were being C batg war wounded.	
	19/7/16		In the morning HQ mess was interfered with very heavily. Shelling forced the Comm of which the adjt Lieut was blown in, the adjutant wounded, and many of the Headquarts papers buried beyond recovery. Means and Cuthbern were rescued.	
	20/7/16		Many Huns planes over the battery position. At 3.25 attack was begun on LONGUEVAL. Iron wire B.75 in MONTAUBAN trenches. Lt Col Cannan found 16 Kl The 6th Div CRA took over own from the 7th CRA Lewars & Cuthbin moved High from E.W.	

WAR DIARY
or
INTELLIGENCE SUMMARY

Army Form C. 2118

(Erase heading not required.)

Place	Date	Hour	Summary of Events and Information	Remarks and references to Appendices
	21st/7/16	6.d.	H.Q.s heavily shelled all afternoon and evening & battery lost 2 killed and 7 wounded. General OUSLEY was wounded in the head by shell in Steele Wood. 2/Lt DUTTON joins the Bn. 2/Lt J.D HINDLEY-SMITH from the 9th Bn. takes over duties of Adjt vice 2/Lt DOBB wounded on the 19th	
	22nd/7/16		H.Qrs heavily shelled in the evening.	
	23rd/7/16		Attack at 1.30 A.M. on SWISS TRENCH. Ordered to move out at 4 P.M. into rest at DERNANCOURT. Relieved at 6 P.M. by 1st & 8th Bn. R.W.F	
DERANCOURT E.16.d & 22	24th/7/16		Col Cardew rejoins the Bn & assumes Command. During the tour in the trenches, 145 positions were work of patrols of two platoons have at the 19th 1st & 22nd. Reinforcements of men and horses arrives and four sent in to Ordnance for repairs	
	25/7/16		General refitting. Carried on in the Bn. 20 remounts received from the D.a.C. to 5 Officers Casualties in personnel amounts to 5 Officers Wounded and 124 O.R. Killed, wounded, and Sick. Horses 32.	

Army Form C. 2118

WAR DIARY
or
INTELLIGENCE SUMMARY

(Erase heading not required.)

Instructions regarding War Diaries and Intelligence Summaries are contained in F.S. Regs., Part II. and the Staff Manual respectively. Title Pages will be prepared in manuscript.

Place	Date	Hour	Summary of Events and Information	Remarks and references to Appendices
SERAINCOURT	Ref map	62 D		
	27/7/16		Inspection of Bde horselines by Maj. Gen Roberts, Comm. 1st division, at 2.30 P.M.	MMG
	28/7/16		Lines visited by A.D.V.S. 53 horses Cast. Present strength of horses 66.	
	29/7/16		In camp at SERAINCOURT, resting and refitting	ditto
	30/7/16		Total expenditure of Ammunition for the Bde since	
	31/7/16		June 24th A 3760 $\qquad$ AX 10897 $\qquad$ BX 13268	
	1/7/16		Total casualties in personnel killed/wounded and	
			wastage from sickness	
			Officers 5. O.Rs 124.	
			horses 32, Cast 53.	

W. J. Jackson
Lt Col R.F.A.
Commdg. R.F.73 Bde R.F.A.

Head Quarters
    17 Divisional Artillery.

Reference G.289 dated 26.7.1916

Following statement as under:-

1. Ammunition Expenditure by Batteries
   from 24/6/16 to 24/7/16
           A.   AX.
   A-80   14,645   4,934.
   B-80   12,411   3,923.
   C-80   10,552   2,030.
                    BX
   D-80   13,268

2. Casualties Killed & Wounded. 24/6/16 - 23/7/16
           Officers   Men   Officers   Men
   A-80 Killed   —   3   C-80 Killed   —   5
        Wounded 2   31   Wounded 1   21
   B-80 Killed   —   7   D-80 Killed   —   1
        Wounded 1   21   Wounded 0   18
   H.Q. Killed   0
        Wounded 1   0

3. Wastage from Sickness 24/6/16 - 23/7/16
   A-80   10   C-80   4
   B-80   2   D-80   1
   Officers nil.

Casualties in Horses 32

30-7-1916   [signature] Lieut Col R.F.A.
                      80th Brigade R.F.A.

17th Divisional Artillery.

80th BRIGADE

ROYAL FIELD ARTILLERY

AUGUST 1 9 1 6

Casualties - Animals.
            Personnel.
Ammunition expenditure.

WAR DIARY or INTELLIGENCE SUMMARY

Army Form C. 2118

80A 80 Vol 14

MAP REF. TRENCH MAP (Erase heading not required.) MONTAUBAN A B C.

Place	Date	Hour	Summary of Events and Information	Remarks and references to Appendices
MONTAU-BAN	1/8/16		Brigade moved into action from BERNAFAY COURT, and took up positions in valley south of MONTAUBAN, A,B,C + and A2A. Major SUTTON R.F.A. took over the Command of the Bde vice Lieut Col Auneil acting C.R.A. Fajub were Bayone on ORCHARD TRENCH. S11C6.9. G/S11C9.8. Heavy hostile shelling during night 1/2. Registered gun during morning. Bombard gun from 6.30 to 7. P.M.	
	2/8/16		Re registered. D battery changed position owing to hostile shelling. A/85 has 2 guns out of action owing action on piston rods.	
	3/8/16			
	4/8/16		Bde bombard 12.35 A.M. to 12.40 A.M. Infantry attack 12.40 AM. A battery 3 guns out of action. C bty 1 gun out of action. Barrage line allied from S11C8.8 - S11a5.7. F.O.O. to be kept with each Hdqs.	
	5/8/16		Quiet day. Guns on SWITCH TRENCH 56a 20.45 - 56a40.70. Ruin of Hostile Balloon observed.	
	6/8/16		Btys heavily shelled on night 5/6th. several dugouts blown in. Lt HOUGHTON casualty from shell shock. Lt CARVER evacuated sick. 4 guns out of action. Casualties C Bty, from 1st to 8/16 Y, O.R. 3 guns. It rained during afternoon.	

WAR DIARY or INTELLIGENCE SUMMARY

Army Form C. 2118

Instructions regarding War Diaries and Intelligence Summaries are contained in F.S. Regs., Part II. and the Staff Manual respectively. Title Pages will be prepared in manuscript.

MAP REF. French Map MONTAUBAN. A.B.C.

Place	Date	Hour	Summary of Events and Information	Remarks and references to Appendices
	7/8/16		Enemy Quieter. Burst of own bombardment from each. Desultory rifle firing all day. Three Phosphorus shells fired over batteries. Bombardment by Bly's 5.30 to 6.30 + double night firing. Bly's H.Q.s heavily shelled during night. Total Casualties 5 k and 9 w. also 3 horses. 9 O.pip.ors in action 16.	
	8/8/16		Bombardment 7.30 to 9.40 AM followed by barrage. Bombardment by Northumberland Fusiliers 5.30 PM, assisted by the Bty.	
	9/8/16		Enemy Quiet. Ordinary day + night firing. Lt Col. Cardew assumed command of Bde.	
	10/8/16		Enemy Quiet. Ordinary day + night firing.	
	11/8/16		Enemy Quiet. 13½ Bty Cents 18 pdr to HEILLY. Expenditure of ammunition from 1st Aug to 10th Aug. A 107 69. BX 26.15. AX 1400.	
	13/8/16		Corps Commander presents MILITARY MEDAL RIBBON to the following 8 n C.O.s and men of the Bde at HEILLY. Enemy a little more active. Bly's firing on enemy's positions.	
	14/8/16 15/8/16		HEILLY + Relieving 22nd Bde + Btys relieved 4 to 10, Enemy O.C.s of the three 5- 6 AM rounded by 8 L.B.	

1875 Wt. W595/826 1,000,000 4/15 J.B.C. & A. A.D.S.S./Forms/C.2118.

WAR DIARY or INTELLIGENCE SUMMARY

Army Form C. 2118

(Erase heading not required) N.Z.A.B.A.N.Z.A.C. 1. 20000 A.3.C.

REF. French

Place	Date	Hour	Summary of Events and Information	Remarks and references to Appendices
MONTAUB-AM	16/8/16		Morning Quiet. Orders received for Bombardment of 17th. Ordinary night firing.	
	17/8/16		Bombardment by all batteries from 6 A.M. to 8 P.M. very slight retaliation. Increased night firing by half.	
	18/8/16		Bombardment from 8 A.M. to Zero hour (2.45 P.M.) Range lengthened by 100 yds owing to successful Infantry attack on ORCHARD trenches.	
	"		New S.O.S. line from S.11.c.3.3 to S.11.c.P.3	
	19/8/16		S.O.S call at 9.15 A.M. lasting for 2 hour owing to slight attack on WOOD LANE.	
AMIENS 17. ALBERT.	20/8/16		Batteries moved out of action at 4.45 P.M. marching independently to BONNAY. 70 Batteries down at positions in time to take over.	
	21/8/16		Divisional Artillery inspected and thanked by Corps Commander Gen. O'C. [?] Shall later in SOMME later.	

Army Form C. 2118

WAR DIARY
or
INTELLIGENCE SUMMARY

(Erase heading not required.) AMIENS Sheet 17. FRANCE 57D 1:20,000 N.E.

Place	Date	Hour	Summary of Events and Information	Remarks and references to Appendices
	22/8/16		Bde moved at 7.30 A.M. from BONNAY to CROISY. Arriving about 11 A.M.	
	23/8/16		Bde marched from CROISY to OUTREBOIS, at 1.45 p.m. Moving at about 7 P.M. Camp & Billets very good.	
HENU D13b. & D13c.	24/8/16		Bde marched from OUTREBOIS to HENU, in new fighting zone starting at 6.30 A.M. and arriving at about 11.30 A.M. All batteries billeted & camped close together.	
	25/8/16		Orders received to the effect that the Bde stand broken up to supply guns & personnel for the forming of 6 gun batteries in the 70th & 79th Fd. Bdes. Bty Commanders taken up to their lines by CRA to reconnoitre positions.	
	26/8/16		Col Cardew proceeds on leave to England. Leaving Capt Craig in command of the Bde.	

Army Form C. 2118

WAR DIARY
or
INTELLIGENCE SUMMARY
(Erase heading not required.)

REF MAP. Sheet 57D N.E. FRANCE Summary of Events and Information 1, 20000

Place	Date	Hour	Summary of Events and Information	Remarks and references to Appendices
	28/8/16		One section from each battery moved into action with the exception of D battery. Remainder for the time being up of the B[?]s were proceeds with.	
	29/8/16		A battery completes the taking up of their positions in the line.	
	31/8/16		Waggon lines of B/s divided and attached to their new Batteries. A B⁴ - R⁺ half to A/78 at GAUDIEMPRE L⁺ " " B/78 " B B⁴ - R⁺ half to C/78 " L⁺ " " A/79 " C B⁴ - R⁺ " " C/79 " L⁺ " " B/79 "	
GAUDIEMPRE D1a + D1b			The taking over of Bys from the 80th Bde by the groups Commanders (O⁺es 78th 79th & 81st Bdys) completes the forming of the 1st Sept /16. The total casualties in the Bde since going into action on the 1st Aug 16 amounted to the following :-	

WAR DIARY
or
INTELLIGENCE SUMMARY

Army Form C. 2118

Officers wounded 2. { Lieut E.S. HOUGHTON
                      { "   A.P. CARVER

Other Ranks. killed 8.
              wounded 16.

Horses killed. 2.
       wounded 2.

Expenditure of ammunition during 1st August to
1st 20th Aug. Date of coming out of action

A   Bx
96453 7158.
       Ax
       6782.

Ministry of ..... to
War.   L' Col Commandt
        80-73d R.F.A.

www.ingramcontent.com/pod-product-compliance
Lightning Source LLC
Chambersburg PA
CBHW051528190426
43193CB00045BA/2374